# Resources

by Michael Teitelbaum

## Table of Contents

# Introduction

A natural resource is something useful we get from nature. Earth has many natural resources. Water, trees, soil, sunlight, and oil are some of them.

We use natural resources every day. We drink water. We use wood from trees to build things. We plant seeds in soil. Heat from the sun helps them grow. We burn oil to heat our houses.

Wood comes from trees.

Plants need water to stay alive.

Earth's natural resources contribute to our lives in many ways. We need soil and sunlight to grow food. We need oil to heat our homes. We need water to keep clean. But all these resources must be used with care.

Plants grow in the soil.

This oil pump works to bring oil out of the ground.

## Chapter 1 Water is Important

Water is important to all living things. People drink and cook with water. They wash clothes and take baths in it. Water helps keep people healthy.

Animals and plants need water. They need it to live and grow.

Where do we find all the water?

**DID YOU KNOW...**

Your body is about 65% water. Your brain is 70% water. Your blood is 82% water, and your lungs are 90% water.

Earth is called the "water planet." Water covers about 70 percent of Earth. 97 percent of this water is salt water. People can't drink salt water. People need fresh water. Only three percent of the water on Earth is fresh.

It is important not to waste our water. In some places water is **recycled**. This means that water is treated so it can be used again.

There's very little fresh water on Earth. We can get fresh water from streams, lakes, rivers, and reservoirs. Some people get fresh water by digging deep holes, called wells, into the ground.

**Language DETECTIVE**

Clue: The subject of a sentence tells what or whom the sentence is about. Find the subject of the last sentence in the text above.

## DID YOU KNOW...

Almost 3 billion people live on Earth without enough fresh water. A lot of water in the world is too dirty to drink.

This girl carries water home to her family in India.

## Chapter 2 Wood is Important

Many common things are made from wood. Wood is used to build houses. Wood is used to make paper for books. Members of baseball teams use bats made from wood!

Where does wood come from?

This machine is making wood chips.

**DID YOU KNOW...**

**Wood chips are soaked in water to create pulp, a mushy material. The pulp is then spread out in thin sheets. When the sheets dry, you've got paper!**

Trees grow in forests. Trees are important to life on Earth.

Trees are an important natural resource. Trees provide some of the oxygen that people need to breathe. Trees put moisture in the air. This moisture causes rain to fall. Many animals make their homes in trees. Trees also give us fruits, nuts, and spices.

Wood comes from trees. Cut trees are taken to a sawmill. There they are cut again into flat boards.

People use the boards, called lumber, to build houses and make furniture.

Trees are also cut down for other uses. Sometimes people cut down trees to clear the land for farming. People also make paper from trees.

Trees are **nonrenewable**. This means they cannot be replaced quickly because they take many years to grow. It is important to plant new trees when old trees are cut down.

Children are donating time to plant a young tree called a sapling. It will take many years to grow large.

## Chapter 3 Soil is Important

Soil is important, too. Soil has the food and water that plants need to grow. Small plants and animals live in the soil.

**Language DETECTIVE** **Clue:** In this sentence, the words "Small plants and animals" are the complete subject. A complete subject includes the subject (plants and animals) and all the words that describe the subject (small). Find the complete subject of the first sentence on page 3.

**DID YOU KNOW...**

You may be unaware that soil comes in different colors. It can be red, yellow, brown, or black.

## DID YOU KNOW...

You can make soil better for planting by adding compost. Compost is made from bits of food, grass, and weeds. Compost adds **nutrients** to the soil. Nutrients are the food in the soil that plants need to grow.

Soil is made up of **minerals**, water, air, and dead plants and animals. Some soil clumps together. Other soil is loose and crumbly. Loose, crumbly soil is best for growing plants.

Soil takes many years to form. This important natural resource must be saved.

## Chapter 4 Oil is Important

What makes a car go? How does a house stay warm? Oil is the natural resource that makes both these things happen. Oil is used to make gasoline for cars, planes, and boats. Oil can also heat a home.

### DID YOU KNOW...

Oil is used to make many things. Plastic, toothpaste, crayons, ink, eyeglasses, and bubble gum are all made from oil.

**Uses of Oil**

|  |  |
| --- | --- |
| Gasoline | 47% |
| Heating Oil and Diesel Fuel | 23% |
| Jet Fuel | 13% |
| Propane | 10% |
| Asphalt | 4% |
| Other Products | 3% |

Machines, called oil pumps, drill to find oil underground. The oil is **refined** into fuel and other items.

Earth's supply of oil is being used up. Scientists are looking for ways to use sun, wind, and water power instead of oil.

## DID YOU KNOW...

Oil comes from the remains of plants and animals. It takes millions of years to form. Oil can't be replaced quickly.

This oil pump is in California. Oil pumps can work all day and all night.

# Conclusion

People use Earth's natural resources every day. Plants and animals need them to live. These important resources shouldn't be wasted.

Scientists are doing research to find new ways to use salt water. They also want to find ways to use less wood.

Scientists are looking for other ways to get **energy**. One day cars might run only on energy from the sun. Our homes may be heated with new kinds of power. Until then, our natural resources must be used with care.

This reservoir in California holds fresh water.

## Glossary

**energy** a force that can make things move ***(page 14)***

**mineral** a substance found in the earth that is not animal or vegetable ***(page 11)***

**nonrenewable** not able to be restored or recovered ***(page 9)***

**nutrient** any substance that nourishes plants or animals to help them grow and be healthy ***(page 11)***

**recycle** to treat something so it can be used again ***(page 5)***

**refine** to change from its original form ***(page 13)***

**reservoir** a large area in which a community's water supply is kept ***(page 6)***

---

## Index

# Comprehension Check

## Summarize

Use the chart to write the main idea and details in this book. Then summarize what you learned about natural resources from this book.

| Detail |
| --- |
| Detail |
| Detail |
| Main Idea |

## Comprehension Check

1. Reread page 8. What is the main idea? What details help you find it? ***(Main Idea and Details)***

2. List some ways that you can help save water. ***(Synthesize)***

3. Why is it important to use our natural resources wisely? Find examples in the text that help you answer this question. ***(Evaluate)***